The way
to school

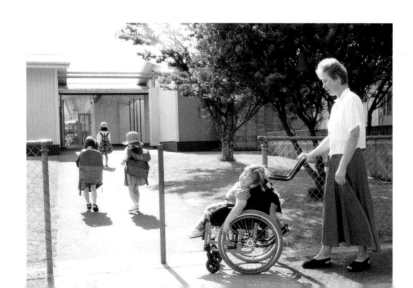

I go to school.

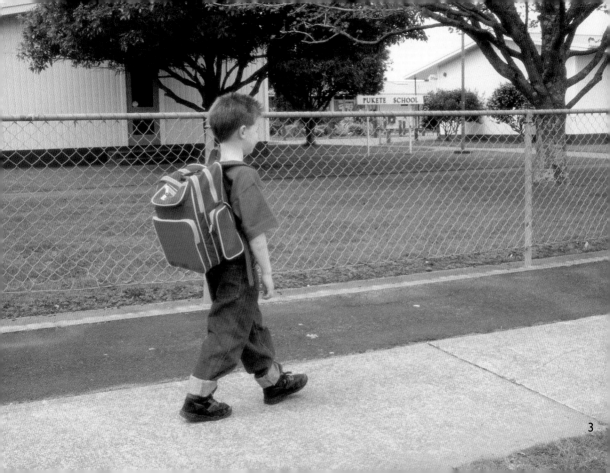

I go to school
in a wheelchair.

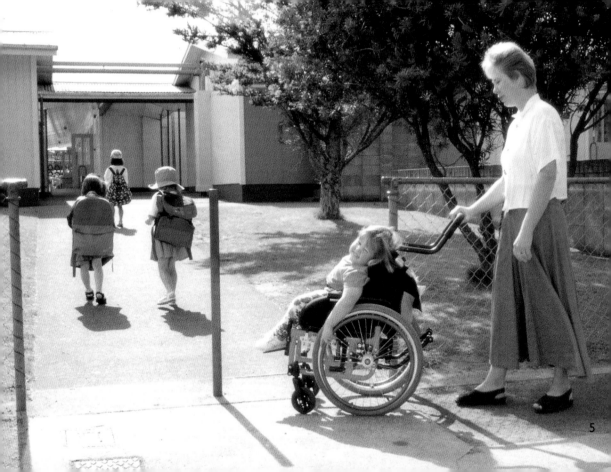

I go to school
on a bike.

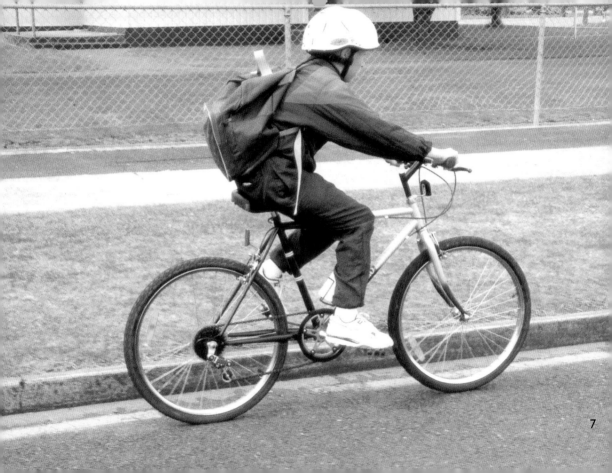

I go to school
in a car.

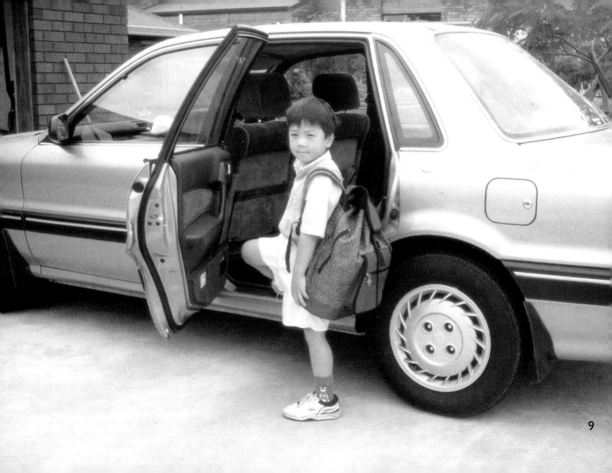

I go to school
in a taxi.

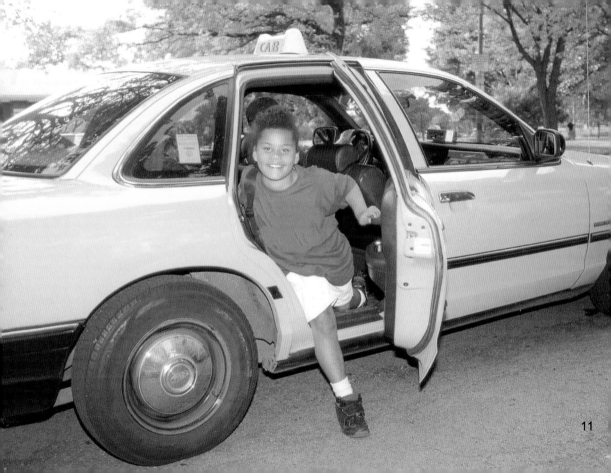

I go to school
in a van.

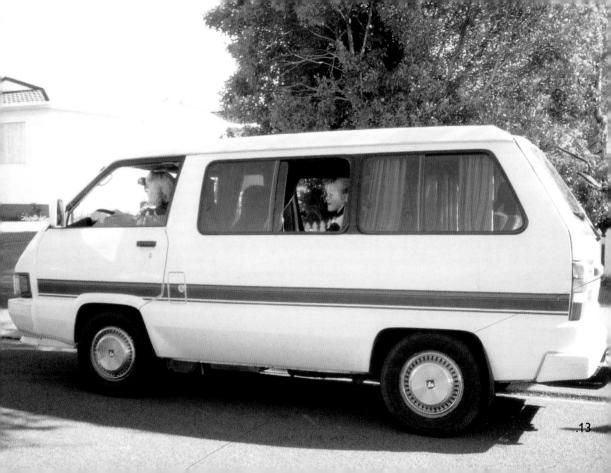

I go to school
in a bus.

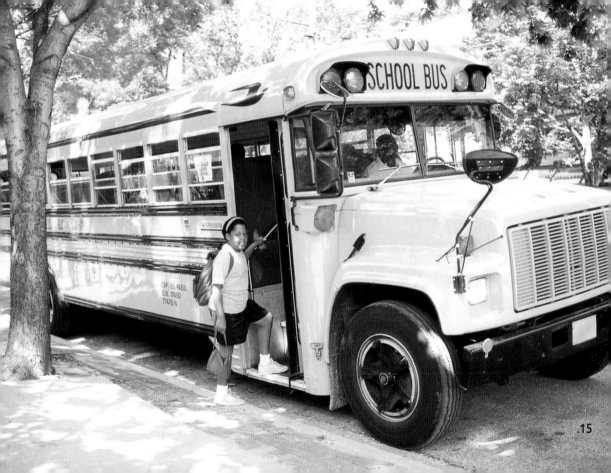

I go to school
on a boat.

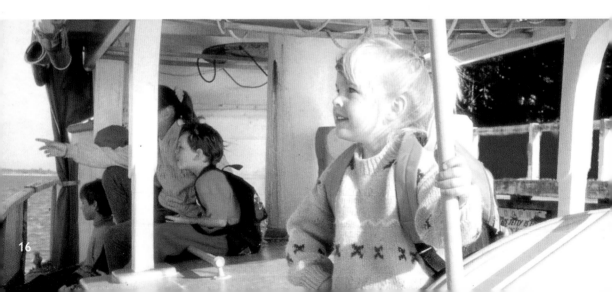